Chinese New Year

by Katie Marsico
illustrated by Holli Conger

Content Consultant: Dr. Pamela R. Frese
Professor of Anthropology, College of Wooster

visit us at www.abdopublishing.com

Published by Magic Wagon, a division of the ABDO Group, 8000 West 78th Street, Edina, Minnesota 55439. Copyright © 2010 by Abdo Consulting Group, Inc. International copyrights reserved in all countries. All rights reserved. No part of this book may be reproduced in any form without written permission from the publisher.

Looking Glass Library™ is a trademark and logo of Magic Wagon.

Printed in the United States.

Text by Katie Marsico
Illustrations by Holli Conger
Edited by Mari Kesselring
Interior layout and design by Becky Daum
Cover design by Becky Daum
Special thanks to cultural consultant David J. Davies, Assistant Professor of Anthropology, Hamline University

Library of Congress Cataloging-in-Publication Data
Marsico, Katie, 1980-
  Chinese New Year / by Katie Marsico ; illustrated by Holli Conger ; content consultant, Pamela R. Frese.
     p. cm. — (Cultural holidays)
  Includes index.
  ISBN 978-1-60270-600-2
  1. Chinese New Year—Juvenile literature. 2. China—Social life and customs—Juvenile literature. I. Conger, Holli, ill. II. Frese, Pamela R. III. Title.
  GT4905.M346 2010
  394.261—dc22
                          2008050547

Table of Contents

What Is Chinese New Year?

Most people in the United States celebrate the New Year on January 1. But for people in some Asian countries, the New Year is different. They celebrate the Lunar New Year, which falls between January 21 and February 19. In China, it is called Chinese New Year.

The date of Chinese New Year depends on the moon. People in China traditionally used a lunar calendar. It is based on the stages of the moon.

Each month on the lunar calendar begins with a new moon. This happens when the earth moves between the moon and the sun. Chinese New Year starts the first day of the lunar calendar's first month. It may be a different date each year. It lasts 15 days.

The beginning of Chinese New Year is based on the stages of the moon. This is also true for the end of the holiday. The full moon lights up the night sky on the fifteenth day of Chinese New Year.

Chinese New Year is about new beginnings. It is a chance for everyone to wish for good luck in the year ahead. People visit with friends and family.

Many people in the United States enjoy this holiday. Some celebrate both Chinese and American New Years. They get two parties!

Chinese New Year is also called Lunar New Year or Spring Festival.

The Story of Chinese New Year

People started celebrating Chinese New Year a long time ago. Old Chinese stories say the holiday started with a terrible dragon named Nian. Nian lived near a small Chinese town. Nian would go to the town on New Year's Eve. He would eat anyone he could find!

An old man knew how to stop the dragon. He told everyone that Nian was scared of the color red, bright lights, and loud noises.

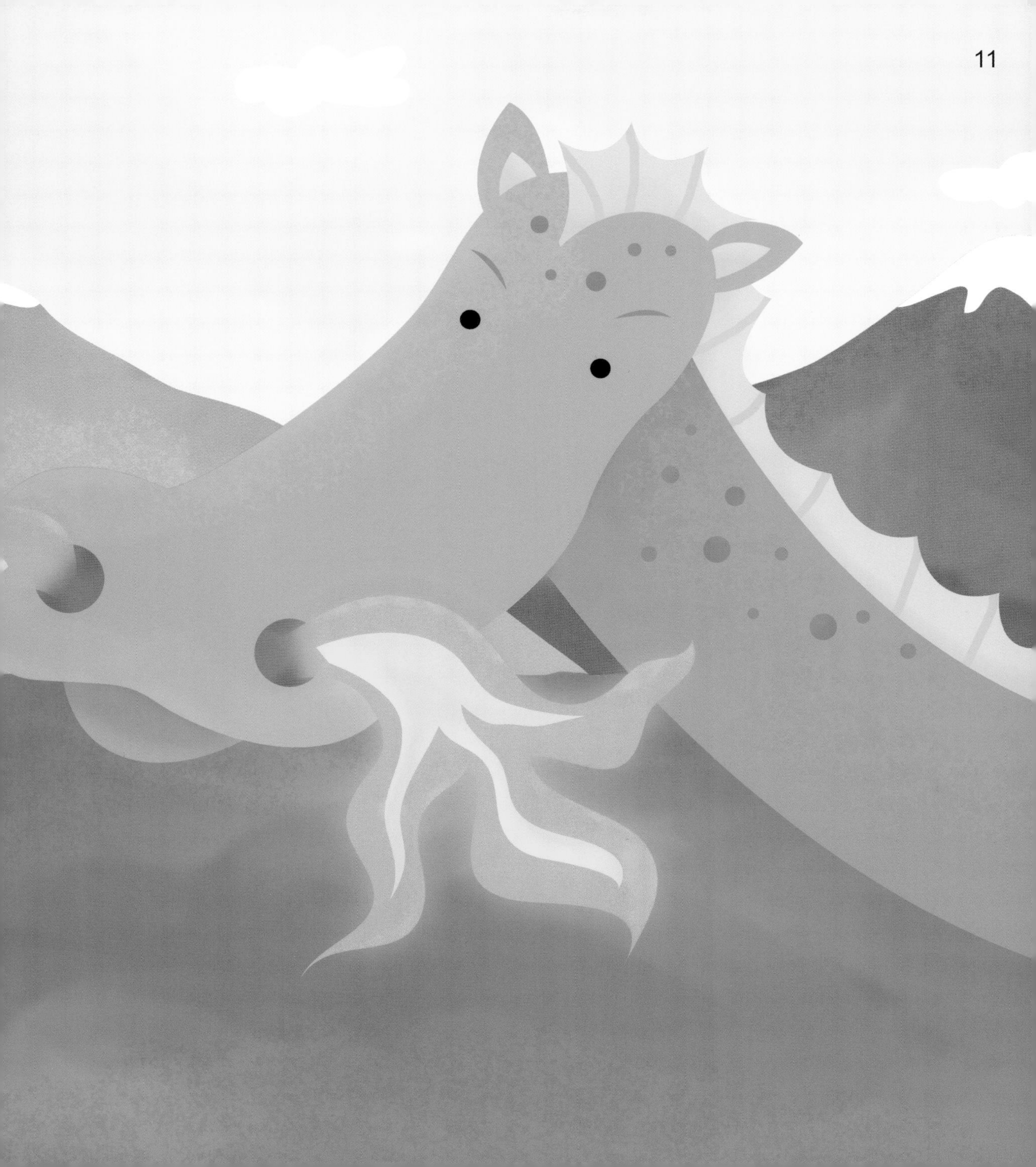

The people in the town listened to the old man. They hung lanterns and red decorations on their houses. They clanged drums and gongs. They even lit firecrackers. It worked. They scared the dragon away!

Nian is an important part of Chinese New Year. Chinese New Year parades often include dragon floats and all the things the people used to scare Nian.

Preparing for Chinese New Year

People prepare for Chinese New Year a week before it begins. They get ready for a year of good luck by cleaning out the old bad luck. They sweep their floors, buy flowers, and repaint their houses.

Some families hang spring couplets, too. These are two-line poems. They are printed on red and gold paper. The couplets are supposed to bring good luck.

Another way to prepare for Chinese New Year is to offer food to the kitchen god. Legend says that this god tells the other gods about the actions of everyone on Earth. Families hope that the kitchen god will say good things about them if they offer treats.

Chinese New Year's Eve is filled with tasty foods. The foods have special meanings. Some families serve a plate of fish. But it is bad luck to eat all the fish. They want to have a little bit left over. This will bring them good luck in the year ahead.

The night ends with a lot of noise. People light fireworks at midnight to scare away evil spirits. They also hope the noise will draw in good spirits. Good spirits can bring happiness.

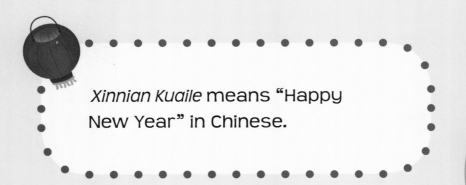

Xinnian Kuaile means "Happy New Year" in Chinese.

Celebrations Today

The morning after Chinese New Year's Eve is exciting. Family members and friends give each other gifts. Children often get red envelopes. The envelopes are called *hong bao*. They have money inside. They are a promise of good luck in the year ahead.

The rest of the day, people visit with family and friends. People also set aside their old clothes. They wear new clothes. This symbolizes saying good-bye to the hardships of last year.

There are many foods to eat during Chinese New Year. At some parties, people share a tray of togetherness. The tray is filled with eight foods. All the foods have different meanings.

- candied melon: growth and good health
- coconut: togetherness
- kumquats: gold and prosperity
- longan: many good sons
- lotus seeds: a large family with several children
- lychee nuts: close family relationships
- peanuts: a long life
- red melon seeds: joy, happiness, and truth

Chinese New Year has a lot of fun events! There are many things to do during the weeks that follow the first day.

Dragon and lion dances are part of the fun. People march in parades. They carry dragon and lion floats. These floats are made from colorful cloth and paper.

On the last day of Chinese New Year, there is a lantern festival. Shop owners hang paper lanterns outside their stores. Sometimes children march around with their own paper lanterns.

The Chinese calendar pairs every year with one of 12 animals. The animals on the calendar are the rat, ox, tiger, rabbit, dragon, snake, horse, ram, monkey, rooster, dog, and pig. Chinese New Year parades often include floats of that year's animal.

People around the world celebrate Chinese New Year. There are many Chinese Americans in the United States. Some larger cities have areas known as Chinatown. These neighborhoods have many Chinese shops and restaurants. They usually have exciting Chinese New Year festivals.

Would you like to celebrate Chinese New Year?

Lion Dance Song

This song is about a lion float in a parade.
Sing this song to the tune of "Mary Had a
Little Lamb."

Lion Dance

See the lion dance and prance
Dance and prance, dance and prance.
See the lion dance and prance
On Chinese New Year's Day.

See the children laugh and clap
Laugh and clap, laugh and clap.
See the children laugh and clap
On Chinese New Year! Hooray!

Chinese New Year Calendar

Chinese New Year falls on a different day each year. This chart shows dates for the first day of the first month on the lunar calendar. This is the date when Chinese New Year begins.

Calendar Year	Date Chinese New Year Begins
2009	January 26
2010	February 14
2011	February 3
2012	January 23
2013	February 10
2014	January 31
2015	February 19
2016	February 8
2017	January 28

Glossary

Chinese lantern—a paper or collapsible covering for a light.

firecracker—a paper tube that holds an explosive, which is set off to make a loud noise.

gong—a disk of metal that makes an echoing sound when struck.

symbol—something that stands for something else.

tradition—customs, ideas, and beliefs handed down from one generation to the next.

On the Web

To learn more about Chinese New Year, visit ABDO Group online at **www.abdopublishing.com**. Web sites about Chinese New Year are featured on our Book Links page. These links are routinely monitored and updated to provide the most current information available.

Index